The Prestige S

South Co

Bob Rowe

Photography by

G H F Atkins

© **2006 R G Rowe & J M Banks**

ISBN-10: 1 905304 11 0/ISBN-13: 978 1 905304 11 9

Cover: Coach and bus building companies were never very numerous in the counties covered by this volume. Kent boasted more than one over the years: the last major one to continue in business was J C Beadle of Dartford. Double-deck bodies by the firm were less than common, but Southdown took twelve on Leyland PD2/12 chassis in 1956. Seen here at Brighton's Pool Valley bus station, **785** (**RUF 185**) was about to depart on service 38 for Bevendean Hospital. The use of the number 38 for this service reflected one of the quirks in the Brighton Area Transport Scheme, for the service had originally been operated by Brighton, Hove & District. Southdown already had a service 38 at the opposite end of its operating territory, used for a route that ran from Portsmouth into the Meon Valley as far as Alton, so for a while it operated two routes utilising this number.

Rear cover: From time to time even the extensive Royal Blue fleet needed to be augmented by hired vehicles and, from the parent fleet, Southern National's No. **404** (**314 EDV**) a Bristol SUL4A delivered in 1960, is seen helping out at Ilfracombe in the summer of 1969.

Inside front cover: East Kent chose the AEC Reliance for its underfloor-engined single-deck bus fleet in 1955, when 40 were delivered with Weymann dual-purpose bodies. Seen at rest at Rye, **KFN 215** and **244** represent the batch. No transport photographer visiting Bournemouth in the 1960s could fail to capture one of the Corporation's elegant Weymann-bodied Sunbeam MF2B trolleybuses. Number **261** (**WRU 261**), seen in Avenue Road, was one of 39 of these fine vehicles.

Inside rear cover: A visit to Teignmouth in 1981 found Devon General's Marshall-bodied Bristol LH6L No. **88** (**VOD 88K**), one of six similar buses delivered in 1972, waiting to depart for Bishopsteignton, a village with a long history of cider making.

Title page: The Daimler CVD6 series was never very common in the south of England, but Exeter Corporation bought 30 in 1948-50, of which six were single-deckers. Number **38** (**JFJ 601**) waits under the red Devon cliffs at Exmouth.

Below: In the postwar period coachwork taken into stock by Maidstone & District was usually from the local builders, Beadle or Harrington. **CO285** (**OKO 33**), however, was a Leyland Royal Tiger with Leyland's own 37-seat body.

>> *Opposite page:* Two of the fascinating coaches to be found at Victoria Coach Station in 1954 were East Kent's **HJG 30**, a very unusual combination of Dennis Lancet UF chassis and Duple Ambassador IV 41-seat coachwork, and a Royal Blue Duple-bodied Bristol LL6B.

Foreword

The rich treasure trove that is Geoffrey (G H F) Atkins's photographic collection tends to concentrate on those locations closer to his home in the East Midlands, but it was clear to the production team at Venture Publications Ltd that sufficient views existed to compile a book in the *Prestige Series* on southern England. As the only 'southerner' in this group, the finger seemed to point to the writer as the person who ought to create this volume. Doing so has been an absolute pleasure, bringing back so many youthful memories and recalling the very first visits made to such counties as Kent and Devon, long before this shy teenager had ever ventured north of Oxford! These visits were made, sometimes complete with ancient fold-out camera, in order to attempt to record the buses that were beginning to gain his interest (much to the consternation it has to be said of his parents!). In no way did the results of these excursions hold a candle to the work of GHFA. So I make no apology for the inclusion of a purely personal selection of this work, but would like to acknowledge and thank - as ever - the skills of John Banks for bringing it to fruition, the support and help of John Senior, not forgetting the invaluable assistance of Mary and David Shaw for trying to keep the writer's sometimes wayward keyboard in check.

Every photograph in the book and on the covers was taken by Geoffrey Atkins and all are © the John Banks Collection.

Bob Rowe
Doncaster
February 2006.

Introduction

One of the most popular series on BBC2 during 2005 was 'Coast'. A panel of experts travelled around part of Britain's coastline each programme visiting areas of particular interest and exploring the history and geography of the location. Long before the BBC decided to commission this series, G H F Atkins had visited many of these places with a view to recording the local transport scene. In this book we follow part of the clockwise journey made by the Television programme, starting in London and following the coast of Southern England from Kent through Sussex, Hampshire, Dorset, Devon and Cornwall and around to Somerset as seen through the camera of Geoffrey Atkins. Those who have read the previous books in the Prestige series will know that the photographer was interested in recording the various types of bus bodywork he discovered. Geoffrey was principally a 'company man' and only two of the previous volumes have been devoted to a municipal fleet: that of Nottingham, his home city. So only scant regard is paid to those fleets which were operated by local authorities in this region and which were once found in Eastbourne, Brighton, Portsmouth, Southampton, Bournemouth, Exeter and Plymouth. With the exception of Eastbourne, all the local authorities were initially tramway operators before their operation eventually became 100% motorbus. But all the photographs, including the small number in colour, are the work of Geoffrey Atkins, from the earliest in 1928 to the most recent used in this book, taken in the 1980s, although it is accepted that there is perhaps a bias to the late 1950s. Geoffrey continued his photography, in a more limited way, right into the 21st century in fact, to the extent that the Guinness Book of Records has recognised this unequalled feat of recording transport subjects during no fewer than nine consecutive decades.

The story concentrates therefore on the large company operators found around the coast of Southern England, principally East Kent, Maidstone & District, Southdown, Devon General, all of which were BET subsidiaries until 1968. There had been early bus operation in all of their areas prior to the First World War; the incidence of the war had led to consolidation of the operations into the companies previously mentioned. In 1929/30 the railway companies took a financial interest in them. The origins of the west country companies of Western and Southern National (owners from 1935 of Royal Blue) and Bristol Tramways was very much involved with the development of the National Omnibus Company and also the railway companies, who from 1929 took a significant financial interest in them. The geographic 'National' names related to the occurrence of either the Southern Railway or the Great Western Railway companies. From 1931 they were associated with the one-time Tilling Empire. From 1969 all of them became National Bus Company subsidiaries, one result of which was to see the Southern National name phased out in favour of Western National. Another change was to see Devon General placed under the control of Western National from 1971. Devon General itself had taken over the municipal system in Exeter in 1970. Today only two former municipal operators remain in local authority control, these being Eastbourne and Plymouth. Unlike the single operator volumes in the Prestige series, no attempt has been made to provide any detail of operator history; indeed, and regrettably, there is not space to include such information. Most of the photographs were taken as a result of holidays in the areas in question and for reasons best known to the photographer, did not include much coverage of Brighton, Hampshire or the Isle of Wight, so unfortunately Brighton, Hove & District, Hants & Dorset, Gosport & Fareham (Provincial) and Southern Vectis are little covered. But for those students of transport all is not lost, for Prestige No. 35 has already been devoted to Hants & Dorset, which covered the segment of the coast from Gosport around to Bournemouth.

The largely rural counties of southern England were not domicile to a great number of coach and bus body building firms, in the way that say, Lancashire, is recognised in this respect. Nevertheless, Kent, Sussex, Hampshire and Devon have been, at one time or another, locations where the construction of such bodywork has taken place. J C Beadle Limited of Dartford has already been referred to in relation to the cover picture, and their products were supplied to all of the BET companies covered by this volume and a few examples are illustrated herein. One speciality of Beadle was its integral single-decker, quite often utilising running units from pre-war AEC and Leyland chassis. Prior to World War II Short Brothers of Rochester were quite prolific, building many bodies under licence from Leyland Motors. Hove, in Sussex, was the home of Thomas Harrington, whose origins went back to the end of the 19th century and who again supplied most of the BET operators covered in this book. There was considerable dismay when, in the mid-1960s, the termination of coach building activities was announced, their Cavalier and Crusader style bodies having been, in the opinion of the writer, amongst the most stylish coach bodies ever produced. Moving east, Wadham Stringer and UVG have carried the torch for Hampshire in recent years, but in the mid-20th century both Readings (of Portsmouth) and Portsmouth Aviation supplied limited numbers of buses and coaches to south coast operators. Regrettably (as far as it has been possible to ascertain), Geoffrey Atkins did not catch examples of either builder on camera. Later in the day Strachans, having been reorganised, decamped to Hamble in Hampshire. Between the wars Mumford was a far-flung outpost of the industry in Devon.

Trolleybus operation, as a successor to tramway operation, was not particularly prevalent in the area under review, although no fewer than four systems did exist along the coast, concentrated two each in Sussex and Hampshire. Purists will probably claim that the number of operators should in fact be five, as at Brighton both the Corporation and Brighton, Hove & District ran them, being an example of the rather rare phenomenon of joint operation of such vehicles, albeit only between 1946 and 1959. A further interesting link between two of the systems was that five of the redundant trolleybuses from Brighton (two municipal and three company) migrated along the coast to Bournemouth in 1959. For the record it should be added that a further small system existed in Maidstone in Kent. All the Hastings trolleybuses had either DY or BDY registration marks, as Hastings was a County Borough, even as far back as Edwardian times, which was when the system of such marks was introduced. In due course when the postwar trolleybuses were sold, the BDY marks appeared in Bradford, Maidstone and Walsall. Other towns in Sussex with County status were Brighton and Eastbourne. In contrast, Kent only had one municipality of County (and indeed City) status - that of Canterbury, which was where East Kent had its head office. East Kent buses, therefore, carried the Canterbury marks of FN and JG whereas Maidstone & District, with a head office in Maidstone, utilised Kent County marks such as KE, KJ, KL, KM, KN, KO, KP, KR and KT. It will be noticed that all three 'phonetic' marks are included in this sequence. It should be noted that where reference is made to the use of particular registration marks on buses in this volume, it relates to the system in use throughout the 20th Century, and not to the nonsense introduced in 2001.

We commence our tour, as did the television programme, in London, with some wonderful views at Victoria Coach Station, a starting point for many holiday makers journeying to the south coast. This area has been a leisure destination for a long time; it was particularly popular with the Victorians and Edwardians, when most significant expansion took place. All of the company operators visited in this book (with the sole exception of Devon General) provided coach services into the capital. In some cases these coaches have been captured in London; in other cases they are found on their home territory. As indicated above, our journey travels firstly to Kent. While the Thanet Coast contained several very popular resorts, it is to the English Channel ports that our first views outside London are found. The Kent countryside has historically been described as the 'Garden of England'; the Channel coast for many centuries was seen as the most vulnerable to invasion from the continent, and fortifications along it reflected this. Indeed, protective measures stretched right along the coast to Portsmouth.

Interestingly, all three of the south-eastern BET companies actually met in Hastings, although no photograph has turned up of all three constituents in one shot.

Our journey then continues along the chalk cliffs of the coast, where along the way three of the municipal operators were to be found, at Eastbourne, Brighton and Portsmouth. As mentioned, those looking for comprehensive cover of them will be disappointed; this is a book of photographs by Geoffrey Atkins, and if he didn't shoot the particular operator and/or vehicle, it will not be found in this book. As also explained, from the western half of Southdown's operating territory around to Bournemouth, photographic coverage is limited. But once into Dorset, whose categorisation as part of the 'West Country'

might be debated, the subject matter more than makes up for this previous shortfall. This is not a geography text book, but pursuing our theme of the BBC Television series, reference is made from time to time to some of the features found in the natural world where our subject matters were based. This applies not least to Devon and Cornwall, which arguably for many years have been among the most popular of tourist attractions in the whole country. The seasonal implications of operation in this environment are hopefully well captured by the selection of photographs and it is expected that for many they will bring back pleasant memories of their own holidays in the West Country.

It is difficult to convey the essence of the raw scenery of the extreme westerly point of England simply by the illustrations and their descriptions; anyone who has visited Lands End in the summer but been refreshed by the wild breeze coming straight off the Atlantic will appreciate the point that is being made. All along the north Cornwall and Devon coastline numerous resorts have retained their popularity over the years; it has only been possible to illustrate a few in this brief survey. Our tour concludes by arriving at the Bristol Channel and the mud flats of the Severn estuary.

By their very nature, coastal resorts attracted holiday makers, whose travel intentions were clearly leisure-orientated. So it was not unusual along the whole of this coast to find at a variety of locations, open-top bus services. Operated almost universally seasonally, they were not all to be found at the same time, and sometimes they ran only for one season; the problems of obtaining a financial return on such a short season mitigating against their continuance. Elsewhere the open-top service virtually became part of the permanent scenery. It is not clear where the first of these services commenced; presumably the thinking was that open-top buses, combined with bracing sea air, would enhance the holiday! One day some author will perhaps produce the definitive book on this fascinating subject. In the meantime only the briefest review of this feature is possible in the space available. One of the features that perhaps made the open-top operation around the coast so fascinating to the enthusiast was the fact that the vehicles that were used were quite often time-expired and therefore suited to late-life conversion and making them of more interest to the enthusiast. The relatively gentle work load they were subsequently to endure was entirely suitable for their new role.

All of the territorial operators represented in this book ran such vehicles at one time or another. No one make of bus had a monopoly on such services. As indicated above, it tended to depend on which buses were coming up for retirement. But their relatively less hectic schedules tended to mean that they stayed in the appropriate fleet longer than their contemporaries. Quite often the only prewar buses still in use to be seen by a young enthusiast in the early 1960s were the open-top ones. Even if they were not quite that old, there was plenty of variety. Among the ranks of such buses were AEC Regents, Bristol Ks, Guy Arabs and Leyland Titans. However, some operators obviously felt that the traffic generated on these services was worth greater investment. That is not to say that open-top vehicles would run all the year round, but

rather that it was worth the investment of purchasing new buses for such operation, buying them with so-called convertible tops so that the roof could be removed for summer operation and refitted for winter use. Brighton, Hove & District was probably the first company in the south to adopt this policy, when they introduced new Bristol FS6Bs in 1960, closely followed by Devon General and the arrival of their 'Sea Dog' class of Leyland Atlanteans in 1961. The naming of such vehicles was not a Devon general innovation - Eastbourne had done the same some years before and Bournemouth was to emulate it subsequently. Southdown's ubiquitous Leyland PD3s included a batch of 25 convertible ones in 1964 and Bournemouth received Daimler Fleetlines in 1965. Even later a batch of convertible Bristol VRs migrated between Southern Vectis and Hants & Dorset.

Certain towns on the coast experienced the luxury of seeing open-top buses operated within their boundaries by more than one operator. Eastbourne, with both Corporation and Southdown, was one; Southdown also

Geoffrey Atkins often travelled by train from Nottingham to St Pancras and then across London to Victoria, sometimes for an onward journey to the South Coast. Arriving at Victoria Southern Region railway station, this was the sort of view that greeted him in the 1950s. If the onward journey was to be by train, then he was on the spot; if by coach, there was a walk of a half-mile or so to Victoria Coach Station. We are fortunate to have Atkins photographs from these London locations.

Geoffrey's Victoria view on page seven is one of a handful of his views that set themselves somewhat apart from his usual portraits of vehicle bodywork by placing vehicles in the context of their operating environment. Geoffrey has said that he would have liked to take more such views but was constrained, as are so many enthusiast photographers, by economics; and, after all, his first love was the art of the coachbuilder, into the recording of which went the bulk of his resources. Few examples of his work are more attractive than this view of the Hastings Tramways open-topped trolleybus No. 3A (DY 4965) among the private cars of the 1940s and 1950s (see also page 20).

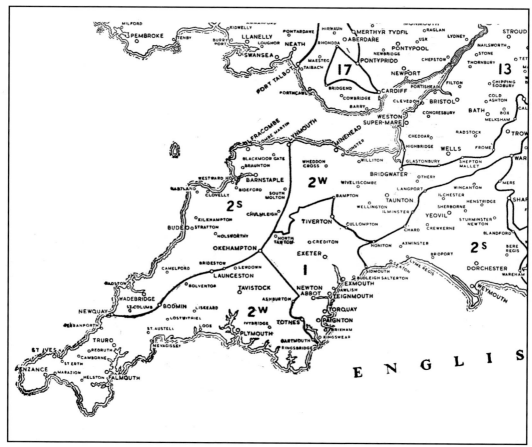

utilised the type in Brighton alongside Brighton & Hove. Bournemouth saw both the Corporation and Hants & Dorset running open-top buses, with the additional benefit that for a few years in the early 1960s the Corporation's examples included trolleybuses, single-deckers and double-deckers all with roofs removed. Hastings too had an open-top trolleybus, but in its case, the vehicle had been so designed from new. Again there were also open-top double-deck and single-deck buses; the latter initially included Dennis Aces, replaced by AEC Regals. In both towns there was clearly an abundance of riches for the enthusiast. For the record, other locations along the south coast that saw the operation of open-top buses included (and the list is not claimed to exhaustive), Hayling Island (Southdown), Portsmouth (Corporation), Isle of Wight (Southern Vectis), Gosport (Hants & Dorset and Gosport & Fareham), Southampton (Corporation), Exmouth and Torquay (Devon General), Plymouth (Corporation), Falmouth and St Ives (Western National) and Weston-super-Mare (Bristol Omnibus). It has been happily possible to illustrate a few examples from this list.

The above notes, necessarily brief, set the scene for the reader to enjoy the benefits of Geoffrey Atkins's excursions 'Down South'.

This map appeared in editions of the ABC Bus and Coach Guide for many years. It showed the approximate areas served by the principal bus operators. As far as this book is concerned, the numbers related to the following operators: 1 Devon General Omnibus & Touring Co Ltd; 2S Southern National Omnibus Co Ltd; 2W Western National Omnibus Co Ltd; 3 Hants & Dorset Motor Services Ltd; 4 Wilts & Dorset Motor Services Ltd; 5 Southdown Motor Services Ltd; 6 Southern Vectis Omnibus Co Ltd; 7 East Kent Road Car Co Ltd; 8 Maidstone & District Motor Services Ltd; 9 Aldershot & District Traction Co Ltd; 10 London Transport.

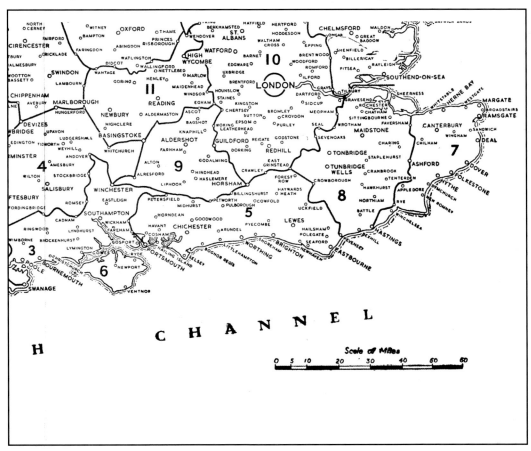

Above: Our tour starts at Victoria Coach Station, where many holidaymakers passed through, and looks at a selection of coaches from the four main express service operators serving the south coast. Passengers from Victoria to Dover in 1935 could have enjoyed the luxury of this Park Royal-bodied Leyland Tiger TS7, **JG 5426**.

Below: Having settled on the AEC Reliance for its coach requirements from 1957, East Kent remained faithful to Beadle for its bodywork order. **MJG 290** represented a design originally developed for the Beadle-Commer integral coach.

Above: Although Maidstone & District, like East Kent, favoured the Leyland TS7 for its coaching requirements in 1935, the former preferred to place its order for coachwork, as shown on No. **592** (**CKE 431**), with Thomas Harrington of Hove.

Below: Nearly 20 years later Harrington was still Maidstone & District's favoured body builder, but by this time Leyland was supplying underfloor-engined Royal Tiger chassis.

Above: Southdown took a large number of Leyland PS1s into stock from 1947 to 1949, with bodies supplied by no fewer than six manufacturers. Fleet number **1240** (**GUF 740**) was one of 25 fitted with Eastern Coach Works bodies (Nos 1227-51); all were downgraded to bus work in 1955 and renumbered 675-699.

Below: Busy summer Saturdays regularly required the use of stage-carriage buses on coach relief work, as demonstrated here by Southdown No. **1504** (**LUF 504**), although it was fitted with dual-purpose seating. Such was the activity at Victoria Coach Station at these times that this 1952 East Lancs-bodied Leyland Royal Tiger had to wait for its return journey outside the coach station.

Above: In 1952 Royal Blue departures from Victoria Coach Station were still very much the preserve of the half-cab coach, although the operator's first underfloor engined coaches did enter service that year. Nearest the camera, No. **1228** (**HOD 30**) is a typical Bristol L6B with Beadle 31-seat body.

Below: The last Bristol LS6G coaches delivered to Royal Blue in 1957 included No. **2205** (**VDV 748**), and although there were only six years between its delivery and that of No. **1268**, an LL6B model on the right, the designs seem a generation apart.

Above: On a staff outing from the then London Transport Country area garage at Godstone is **RF46** (**LYF 397**), seen here at Dover in July 1952. As a Green Line coach it would have been ideal for the run down the A2 to the coast. The RF was based on the AEC Regal IV with 39-seat body supplied by Metro-Cammell and this example was new in 1951.

Below: **JG 6820** was a Dennis Lancet delivered in 1936 and was one of a large batch, numbering 26, of the first such buses taken into stock by East Kent. The bodywork, which closely resembled contemporary Park Royal designs, was actually built by the chassis maker. When new JG 6820 was fitted with a petrol engine, but this was fairly soon replaced by a diesel unit. The company was somewhat unusual in that for many years no fleet numbers were allocated, the registration number being utilised to identify each vehicle.

From 1936 to 1938 East Kent took into stock no fewer than 75 Leyland TD4s and TD5s with either Brush or Park Royal bodies, all instantly recognisable by their 'JG' registrations. In our first visit to Folkestone there is the opportunity to see what became of these buses after the war. Some of the TD4s, such as **JG 8231**, *(upper picture)* received new Eastern Coach Works 55-seat lowbridge bodies in 1948. Most of the remaining TD4s and the TD5s, such as **JG 9913** *(lower picture)* received new lowbridge bodies from Park Royal. The views date from July 1952.

Above: **BFN 797** was the last prewar single-decker taken into stock, although it actually arrived in 1940. It was intended to be the forerunner of a fleet of such coaches, but the outbreak of war put a stop to that. The Park Royal-bodied Leyland Tiger TS8 is also seen in Folkestone in the summer of 1952.

Below: Although East Kent was obliged to take into stock large numbers of Guy Arab double-deckers during the war, 65 in fact being delivered, its first postwar double-deckers reverted to Leyland. As we shall see, however, the company was to return to Guy. **CJG 985** was a 1948 Leyland PD1A with Leyland 53-seat lowbridge body, one of 49.

Although the map on page nine clearly shows Folkestone to be well and truly inside East Kent's operating area, the lengthy service 10, jointly operated between Maidstone and Folkestone by East Kent and Maidstone & District, brought the latter's buses to this part of the Kent coast. Conversely, East Kent buses would be found in Maidstone. In the upper view, the Maidstone company's partiality for the Bristol K6A model between 1944 and 1949 is demonstrated by **DH243 (JKM 940)**. The majority of the Bristols were bodied by Weymann, in some cases replacement bodies being supplied by the same body builder as we shall see. DH243, however, was the final bus in an order for 40 supplied by Saunders Engineering in 1948. The lower view shows **DH403 (NKT 899)**, a 1951 Leyland PD2 with classic Leyland Farington body. Behind the Leyland, one of East Kent's many Park Royal-bodied Dennis Lancets awaits to depart for Dover. In later life, many of these Lancets were rebuilt with fully fronted forward entrances to make them suitable for one-man-operation.

Above: No doubt about the location of East Kent **EFN 560**, a 1949 Dennis Falcon 20-seat bus. The impressive viaduct in the background was originally part of the South Eastern & Chatham Railway, but at the time of the photograph was carrying the Southern Region's line. At one time Folkestone was the English port for boat trains to France.

Below: Reference has already been made to East Kent being obliged to take Guy chassis during the war. After an initial batch of postwar Leylands, the Guy Arab was the only chassis purchased for double-deck requirements from 1950 until 1957. **EFN 174**, also seen in Folkestone, was representative of the first batch of Guy Arab/Park Royal units delivered in 1950. These were of lowbridge layout; all subsequent Guys were highbridge. These July 1952 views in Folkestone pre-date the town's modern bus station by three years.

Moving along the coast across Romney Marsh and into East Sussex, we come to Rye, one of the Cinque Ports dating back to the 13th Century. Not quite as old, but certainly as interesting *(above)*, was Maidstone & District **SO68 (RKE 540)**. In a fleet where one-offs were rare, this Saunders-Roe integral single-decker, with Gardner 5HLW engine, was to remain unique. Also to be found in Rye in August 1956 *(below)* was **DH120 (HKE 221)**, one of 63 Bristol K6As delivered in 1944/5. All were rebodied by Weymann between 1951 and 1954; the earlier ones received bodies as seen on page 22, but DH120 was dealt with at the time the Orion style was being produced. Progress is not always for the better.

Above: The guidebooks will tell you that you are now in 1066 country. Hastings was one of those towns where all three BET subsidiaries based in Kent and Sussex met, to say nothing of the provision of a trolleybus network as well. Hastings Tramways No. **3A (DY 4965)** was a remarkable vehicle, seen here in 1956, having been used to open the system in 1928. Replaced by war-time vehicles, this Dodson bodied Guy BTX owed its survival to the fact that it became an overhead greasing vehicle. It was open-topped from new, and re-entered service in Coronation Year 1953 on a seasonal service between the Fishmarket and Bathing Pool.

Below: Considering the amount of coastline served by Maidstone & District, it is perhaps surprising that its only open-top double-deck buses were also to be found in Hastings. **OT5 (FKO 229)** was a 1939 Leyland TD5 with 48-seat Weymann body. The vehicle was another delivered new as an open-topper. It is parked in Wellington Square, where the topography was perhaps less than ideal for a bus terminus.

Above: Also to be found at the Hastings terminus in Wellington Square and again demonstrating the significant gradient on which the buses were parked was Southdown No. **230 (FUF 230)**, visiting from Eastbourne. It was a Leyland TD5 new in 1938 and rebodied in 1950 by East Lancs.

Below: Wellington Square was also the location for this photograph of Maidstone & District **DH482 (VKR 474)**, a 1956 AEC Regent V. By this time the company was favouring Park Royal for its double-deck bodies and DH482 was photographed in the summer it was new.

Above: Besides linking the West Country with the capital, Royal Blue coaches could be found along the length of the South Coast. This view of Royal Blue No. **1293** (**OTT 92**), a 1953 Bristol LS6G, incorporated a roof box in its 41-seat Eastern Coach Works body that was by this time a feature unique to Royal Blue coaches. It was found at Bexhill in August 1956 in less than clement weather. Since Royal Blue was a trading name only, all coaches were nominally owned by either Western or Southern National, the latter in the case of No. 1293.

Below: Maidstone & District **DH123** (**HKE 224**) was outside the company's garage in Bexhill in this 1956 photograph. It was one of the large number of Bristol K6As rebodied by Weymann; it was dealt with in 1952 and thus received a much more attractive four-bay body than sister vehicle DH120 shown on page 19. In the background is another Bristol K6A.

Above: In 1946/7 Maidstone & District took delivery of a further 41 Bristol K6As, of which **DH191** (**HKR 43**) was one, but this time the original classic Weymann 56-seat bodies were retained throughout their life with the Maidstone company.

Below: Still in Bexhill, **DH484** (**VKR 476**), another of the Park Royal-bodied AEC Regent Vs was operating on joint service 15, en route for Eastbourne, with the English Channel in the background. These were the last AEC double-deckers purchased, orders from 1959 being for the PDR1/1 model supplied by Leyland, as seen on page 53.

Above: In 1955 Maidstone & District chose the AEC Reliance for its coach fleet and seen outside Bexhill West Station is **CO315** (**TKM 315**), which was fitted with a Harrington 37-seat body. Maidstone & District remained loyal to either Beadle or Harrington for nearly all its coach bodies from 1946 until 1966.

Below: Heading back towards home territory was Southdown No. **165** (**EUF 165**), a 1937 Leyland TD5 with 1949 Park Royal body. It is also seen on the jointly operated service 15, which linked the two coastal resorts every half hour at this time.

Above: The Hastings Tramways Company was a statutory undertaking which commenced operating trams in 1905. Trolleybuses replaced the trams in 1928/9 and the company was acquired by Maidstone & District in 1935. Trolleybuses ran for the last time in May 1959. Seen here near Bexhill Station under classic trolleybus overhead, No. **32** (**BDY 807**) was a 1947 Sunbeam W with Weymann body. After the closure of the system, it travelled the short distance to Maidstone, where it continued in service until December 1965.

Below: The furthest point west reached by Hasting's trolleybuses was Cooden Beach, where No. **33** (**BDY 808**) is pictured turning. It was later to run in Walsall, along with seven more of the Sunbeams, where they ran until 1970. Both the views on this page date from August 1956.

<< *Opposite page:* In a shot perhaps typifying the villages once served by Southdown, No. **271** (**GUF 671**), a 1946 Leyland PD1 with Leyland's own bodywork, had stopped in Westham, near Pevensey, in order to pick up passengers for points to Eastbourne. Thanks to the forethought of the photographer, who included the sign post on the B2191, we know that the bus had four miles to travel to Eastbourne and that Hastings was twelve miles in the opposite direction.

Above: Eastbourne No. **2** (**JK 6711**) was one of five Leyland TD5cs, with Leyland's own bodywork, delivered in 1937. The wartime restrictions on visits to the coast, and the subsequent reduction in traffic, consequently saw this bus loaned to Lancashire United from 1942 to 1944. Its torque converter was removed and a Leyland diesel engine fitted in 1952; four years later, and the year in which it is seen here, it was converted to open-top form, in which condition it ran until 1963. It was named White Rose.

Below: Eastbourne was one of those coastal towns in which more than one operator provided open-topped buses on tourist-orientated routes. Southdown No. **446** (**GUF 146**), delivered in 1944 with Park Royal utility bodywork, was converted to this form in 1954 and is seen here about to commence the long climb up to Beachy Head.

At the time of rapid bus service expansion, it seemed that no self respecting town should be without its own bus station. Generally used for out-of-town bus and coach services, Eastbourne's example opened in 1927. In these 1956 views, the upper one shows Southdown No. **538** (**PUF 638**), a 1956 Park Royal bodied Guy Arab, with a utility bodied Guy hiding in the interior. The lower view shows two Leylands, Nos. **386** (**JCD 86**) and **250** (**GCD 350**). The former was a 1948 PD2/1 with Leyland body; the latter a 1939 TD5 with 1949 Park Royal body.

Above: Beachy Head is perhaps one of, if not the, most distinctive locations on the whole of the south coast. Geologists will tell us that the chalk cliffs, found throughout Kent and Sussex, were formed 100 million years ago and stand 540ft above sea level. (Southdown's advertising department added another 60 ft, however!) Southdown No. **444** (**GUF 144**), another Guy Arab converted to open-top, prepares to return to Eastbourne.

Below: Approaching the bus terminus and making a spirited climb up the cliffs is 1948 Park Royal-bodied Leyland PS1/1 No. **1305** (**HUF 305**). Similar coaches were to be found in the East Kent fleet.

Upper: Brighton's Pool Valley bus station was a mecca for enthusiasts, but often gave photographers lighting difficulties. In this October 1965 view two Southdown Leyland Titan PD2/12s stand in the autumn sunlight. On the left is No. **729** (**LUF 229**), which had a Leyland body; No. **774** (**OCD 774**) on the right was bodied by Park Royal.

Lower: Brighton in June 1972, with the railway station in the far background. Vehicles of all three local fleets are shown, although by this time Brighton, Hove & District had come under Southdown control following the formation of the National Bus Company three years earlier. It still came as a shock to see Brighton Corporation vehicles in the new blue livery, introduced about a decade earlier.

We have already seen one example of a London Transport bus on a visit to the coast for the benefit of the staff, and in these two photographs, nestling among assorted Hants & Dorset Bristols of types K6A, LL6B and FS6G at Bournemouth bus station are two more, **RT2125** (**KGK 934**), probably from Rye Lane, Peckham Garage, and **RT1639** (**KXW 261**), from Merton Garage. The K6As in the pictures commenced their working lives in London, being allocated to London Transport when new in 1948/9 to meet a postwar shortage of buses in the Capital. At the time the photographs were taken, Bournemouth was most definitely in Hampshire, but is now in Dorset, as a result of Local Government boundary changes 1974.

Above: Bournemouth Corporation's second batch of underfloor-engined single-deckers were Leyland Tiger Cubs with Park Royal bodies delivered in 1955. The first of these, No. **95** (**RRU 900** - numbered 263 when new) is seen here in Bourne Avenue, waiting to depart on the eight-minute journey to Bourne Valley Road on service 19.

Below: In 1965 Bournemouth took delivery of 20 Daimler Fleetlines with bodies by Weymann, The first ten had detachable roofs to allow them to be operated as open-topped buses in the summer. Number **183** (**CRU 183C**) is seen at Alum Chine soon after delivery and is about to depart on the cliff-top journey to Hengistbury Head. Bournemouth also gave their open-topped buses names; here they were named after counties and 183 was Staffordshire.

Above: This view, taken at Bournemouth Pier in 1966, is at a location that, like many others in this book, has changed much in the last 40 years. In the case of this picture, not the least of the changes was the removal of the trolleybus overhead in 1969. Bournemouth No. **101** (**CRU 101C**) was one of three Leyland Leopards which entered service in 1965, with coach seating in their Weymann bus shells. It was about to depart on an inter-pier service to Boscombe.

Below: Some 15 miles along the coast the chalk has well and truly been left behind and we have reached the Isle of Purbeck and the eastern end of the so-called Jurassic Coast, which has been designated a UNESCO World Heritage site. Unlikely to have ever acquired any similar status was Hants & Dorset No. **679** (**KEL 407**), seen here at Swanage. Originally a 1950 Bristol L6G fitted with a Portsmouth Aviation coach body, in 1961 this was removed, the chassis lengthened and rebuilt, thus becoming an LL6B with a new ECW 39-seat bus body.

Above: Weymouth was the most westerly location in which Hants & Dorset buses could be seen. Here they met the local operator Southern National. Double-deck buses of both fleets were originally painted in Tilling green with two cream bands; it is rumoured a senior Tilling officer ordered the removal of one of the bands on Hants & Dorset vehicles in order to be able to identify vehicles from the respective fleets. Representing our Weymouth view is this diminutive Western National Bristol SU No. **424 (274 KTA)**.

Below: At one time Devon General buses also reached Weymouth, but the most westerly view we have in this collection is at Lyme Regis. This wonderful May 1937 view portrays Harrington-bodied Leyland Tiger TS7 **BDV 5**, new the previous year and replete with sunshine roof and sliding door. Decorations are in place for the Coronation of George VI; the photographer was *en route* for Lands End on a Barton Coach Tour. BDV 5 was to be requisitioned by the War Department three years later; it was returned to Devon General ownership in 1943 and in 1948 it passed to Ribble Motor Services.

Above: Moving on into Devon, Sidmouth was yet another town where vehicles from two operators met. Accompanied by a Devon General double-decker, Southern National No. **309** (**DDV 36**), a prewar Bristol L5G with a postwar Beadle body, waits to return to Lyme Regis. Note the via blind - yes, there really is a village called Beer.

Below: The Devon General bus was No. **733** (**PDV 733**), a so-called tin-fronted AEC Regent with Weymann Orion body new in 1954. Devon General was an early user of lightweight double-deck bodies, taking the prototype Weymann Aurora in 1952.

Above: Sister Southern National Bristol L5G No. **310** (**DDV 37**) ,was also in use on service 45 at Sidmouth in 1955 when captured by the photographer. This time the via blind is set for rather less appealing intermediate points.

Below: Another reminder that Royal Blue coaches could be found throughout the length of the South Coast finds No. **1213** (**JUO 978**) caught in Exmouth, about to set off for Bournemouth, the hub of Royal Blue operations. The Bristol L6B chassis was fitted with an attractive body by Beadle and was later to be provided with a new Eastern Coach Works bus body, suitable for one man operation.

In 1934/5 Devon General acquired its first diesel-engined buses, Nos. 200-223 (OD 7487-7510), 24 AEC Regents which were used to replace Torquay's trams. In 1955 six of them were rebuilt by Longwell Green of Bristol to open-top form, and **OD 7505** is seen here in Exmouth *(above)*. A further 13 of the batch had new Brush bodies fitted in 1949 and **OD 7507** is also seen at Exmouth, at the Railway Station yard *(below)*. Both were photographed in July 1955; the closed-top buses were to last for two more years and the open-toppers until 1961. Geologically, Exmouth is regarded as the western end of the Jurassic Coast.

Devon General's first AEC double-deckers after the war were eight RT-type Regents. It must have been a hot July day in 1955 when **HTT 328** was captured at Exmouth waiting to depart to Littleham Village. In the writer's opinion the classic lines of the Weymann four-bay body have never been bettered and justify the inclusion of both off-side and near-side views. The latter clearly shows the lower bonnet line of the RT-type when compared with other Regents. Although not visible in the photo, where the London Transport badge would have graced the top of the radiator, a special 'D G' badge was fitted for these provincial buses.

Above: Also to be found in Exmouth, as a result of the 1947 coordination agreement between Exeter Corporation and Devon General, was the former's No. **36** (**JFJ 58**), a Brush-bodied Daimler CVD6 of 1948. It is about to leave on the long cross-county service 85 to Crediton, on which Corporation operation commenced following the establishment of the wide-ranging coordination area agreement.

Below: At Crediton in 1931 the photographer found this almost brand new Devon General Leyland LT5, which was fitted with a 31-seat Weymann body, parked in the centre of the High Street, the virtual dearth of traffic permitting such a venture. The bus was to be withdrawn in 1938 and was subsequently to be used as a lorry.

Above: Exeter Corporation No. **36** (**FJ 7834**) was also virtually brand new when captured proceeding along Exeter High Street in 1931. By sheer coincidence it is just about to pass the Home & Colonial Stores where the writer's father once worked in the 1920s. The vehicle was a Leyland TD1 with Brush 48-seat body and its entry into service enabled the city to dispense with its trams.

Below: Paul Street Exeter, where the country services terminated, was the location of the bus station in use from 1930 until replaced by the Paris Street facility, approximately a mile away across the city centre, in July 1964. By arrangement with Exeter City Council, all the country services terminated here. In this 1937 view an assortment of Devon General Leylands and a Royal Blue coach are visible.

Above: Parked on the next level down at Paul Street bus station from the picture opposite, **OD 2294** was one of 21 Weymann-bodied Leyland LT5s taken into stock in 1932, all of which were withdrawn by 1940.

Below: Devon General's first diesel-engined saloons comprised a batch of no fewer than 48 Leyland LT7s with extremely attractive Harrington 36-seat bodies, delivered in 1937. Unlike on the earlier Harrington-bodied Tigers, there was no sunshine roof and the doors were of the folding variety. They were, however, fitted with a side destination box, which tended not to be used in later years, although as **CTA 107**, seen at Paul Street, was almost new when photographed, it is perhaps not surprising to note the Okehampton display. Final withdrawals of the batch were made in 1951.

Above: In 1937/8 five AEC Regents fitted with the first metal-framed bodies for Devon General entered the fleet. The Weymann bodies were equipped with a new style of destination box which projected considerably from the front of the bus. **ETT 997** was to last until 1956, the year after this photograph was taken.

Below: Delivered in 1939, **DDV 421** was originally an AEC Regal with a Harrington single-deck bus body. In 1953 around 20 similar chassis, including this one, were rebuilt and rebodied with Weymann Orion bodies as seen here two years later. Both buses were parked at Paul Street.

Above: Wartime deliveries were largely comprised of Guy Arabs with utility bodies of inferior quality. Accordingly, 15 Weymann-bodied Arabs of 1943/4 were rebodied by Roe in 1951. **JTA 312**, along with seven others, also had platform doors fitted by Roe two years later. All were withdrawn by 1960.

Below: Although the Head Office of Western and Southern National was situated, until 1961, at Queen Street (which ran across the top of Paul Street) near Exeter Central Station, incursion into the city by their buses, apart from the Royal Blue services, was extremely limited. Southern National No. **1836** (**LTA 946**), a Bristol KS5G, lays over at Paul Street during a break operating service 47 from Weymouth.

Above: Devon General took a large number of AEC Regals with Weymann bodies into stock from 1946 to 1950. Representative of these in this 1955 Paul Street view were **LUO 597** and **HUO 525**. Exeter Corporation took almost identical bodies on six Daimler CWD6s in 1950.

Below: A last look at Exeter depicts the final batch of AEC Regent IIIs delivered to Devon General, with exposed radiators and traditional Weymann bodywork, although by this time to 8ft-wide specification, and shows **NTA 666** of 1952, together with the new order (i.e. underfloor-engined) as far as single-deckers were concerned, in the shape of Leyland Royal Tiger **MTT 635** of 1950, fitted with Willowbrook 43-seat bodywork. This style of body was to remain the standard for underfloor single-deckers until 1961.

Moving down the coast, yet another estuarial location is reached; after the Exe comes the Teign, and the ancient port and market town of Teignmouth. Two of Devon General's ubiquitous Weymann bodied AEC Regents of the **MTT** series pause while passing through on the Dawlish - Newton Abbott service; judging by the queues in the upper photograph, business was good.

Above: This view in Torquay, at one time termed the English Riviera, offers proof that holidays in Devon were not always blessed with fine and dry weather. **OD 9488**, a 1934 Leyland Lion LT5 with Brush body, is about to travel a few miles down the coast to Paignton in this 1937 view.

Below: A more modern view of Torquay, taken in 1985, shows a Devon General Bristol VR/ECW of 1971, **ATA 554L**, in the final days of the National Bus Company.

For once our tour along the southern coast of England glimpses a well known resort in more recent times. This volume is not the place to discuss the merits or otherwise of the 1980's minibus revolution (initially introduced by Devon General in Exeter in 1980), but these two views show the impact of the introduction of minibuses in Paignton, trading under the Bayline local identity. Although the Ford Transit chassis seen in 1985 were standard, bodies were by Carlyle and Robin Hood.

Above: A short distance along the coast is yet another Devon River, the Dart. This 1981 view of Dartmouth shows an unidentified Western National Bristol VR double-decker mixing with the marina activity in the heyday of the National Bus Company. Not far away the now preserved former Great Western Railway line curves around the coast back to Paignton.

Below: A final look at Devon General found the photographer at Bretonside bus station in Plymouth in 1967. A 1965 AEC Regent V with front entrance Park Royal body, **CTT 511C**, was waiting to return to Torquay on service 128. Unfortunately for us, the photographer did not ascend the stairs at the bus station to capture any of the buses of Plymouth Corporation, whose extensive fleet totalled in excess of 250. A coordination agreement between the Corporation and Western National predated the Exeter agreement by some five years.

>> *Opposite page:* The final county encountered on our journey west is Cornwall, where the red sandstone of Devon has been replaced by dark granite; moving into the Duchy, our first call is at the cathedral city of Truro. Geoffrey Atkins's 1937 holiday has provided a rich vein of material, none better than this Western National Leyland Lion, No. **1047** (**UO 7160**), rebodied by Mumford. For the uninitiated, Simonds, whose beer was found extensively throughout the West Country, had their original brewery located in Reading.

Above: Almost due south of Truro is Falmouth, which contains the 3rd largest natural deep-water harbour in the world. Western National No. **1071** (**BFJ 171L**), one of 17 Bristol VRTSL6Gs delivered in 1971 with Eastern Coach Works 75-seat bodies of standard NBC style, is seen here in the town.

Below: Also found by the photographer in Falmouth, and for use on less heavily trafficked routes (and out of the summer season there were quite a few of these), was one of the compact Western National Bristol LH6Ls, No. **1600** (**NFJ 600N**), one of 50 delivered between 1970 and 1975.

Above: Capital of the far west of Cornwall is Penzance, situated on Mounts Bay and dominated by Mount St Michael. It was the terminus of the Great Western Railway (later the Western Region of British Railways) from Paddington. As it has the most westerly major harbour on the English Channel, it is from here that ferry services to the Isles of Scilly depart. Western National's depot in Penzance was situated at the quaintly named Wherry Town, and this rather unusual view by Geoffrey Atkins captures all the aspects of a country town depot.

Below: Western National No. **2804** (**GFJ 668N**) was one of the company's first Leyland Nationals, delivered in 1974 and also seen here at Penzance.

Above: Western National No. **1068** (**BFJ 168L**), photographed in Penzance in September 1980, was running under the local identity fleetname Cornish Fairways.

Below: Western National No. **1556** (**FDV 786V**) was one of a small batch of short Eastern Coach Works-bodied Bristol LHs, new in 1980 and allocated to Penzance depot for use on some particularly tortuous routes.

Above: Alongside Leyland National **2804** in this 1980 view in Penzance is Western National No. **996** (**521 DKT**), a Leyland PDR1/1 that had been new to Maidstone & District in 1959. That the company had need to operate second-hand 21-year old buses was perhaps indicative of the somewhat precarious operating margins in this part of the country.

Below: Western National No. **1557** (**FDV 787V**) is seen at the other end of service 508 in Mousehole, a picturesque fishing village which history records was sacked by the Spanish in 1595. The photographer annotated the reverse of this print 'a tight squeeze'. Indeed!

Above: Ten miles from Penzance lies Lands End, the most westerly point in mainland England. Here the jagged granite rocks that slope into the Atlantic form a final full stop. It is the most visited outdoor attraction in the county. Western National's 1978 open-top Bristol VR **VDV 144S**, new in 1978, was waiting to leave on the service to St Ives in this 1980 view.

Below: Waiting to head back to Penzance, another Western National Bristol VR, this time roof-equipped, No. **1070** (**BFJ 170L**) was parked with the First and Last House in England in the background.

Above: We move back into Devon with a visit to Lee, a village two miles west of Ilfracombe. During his holiday in the extremely picturesque village in June 1932, Geoffrey Atkins captured this view of Western National Strachan-bodied AEC Reliance **DR 5112**, a vehicle that had been new in 1929.

Below: Moving on to Ilfracombe, situated right on the edge of the Bristol Channel, this evocative view from June 1931 sees Southern National No. **3337 (DR 9988)** heading out to perhaps one of the most imaginatively named places on the north Devon coast, Westward Ho! This Strachan-bodied Leyland Titan was new in 1929.

Above: Although Ilfracombe had first been developed as a tourist resort in the 1880s, aided by the arrival of the railway, the expansion of express coach services in the 1920s and 1930s gave the industry further impetus. In May 1931 Bristol Greyhound commenced a joint service (with the Merseyside Touring Co.) to Liverpool. Bristol B-type **HW 4506** was leaving Ilfracombe in the very early days of the service.

Below: Still in Ilfracombe, Southern National No. **2906** (**DR 5197**), an all-Leyland double-decker of 1929, was taking on a good load for its trip to Combe Martin. The poster in the front window promotes the local Shopping and Fashion week in June 1931.

Above: Strachan-bodied AEC Reliance No. **2877** (**DR 5277**) of Southern National was also operating on the service to Lee (see page 55) in this 1931 view, but this time was captured at the Ilfracombe end of the route. It will be noticed that most of the previous North Devon-based National vehicles illustrated carried DR registrations - prior to the establishment of the Western and Southern National companies in 1929, with a head office in Exeter, the National company used Plymouth marks. DR had in fact originally been allocated to Devonport.

Below: A final look at Ilfracombe: the bus station in August 1962 was host to visiting coaches and a representative collection of Southern National vehicles.

Above: Moving yet further along the north Devon Coast we come to Lynmouth, on the edge of Exmoor National Park, and at the point where the River Lyn flows into the Bristol Channel. Caught in the coach park one summer's day in August 1962 was two-year-old Bristol SUL4A No. **400** (**334 EDV**), the first Bristol SU to enter the Western National fleet. Alongside is No. **430** (**280 KTA**), then only recently delivered. The subtle changes to the style of the coach bodies over two years by Eastern Coach Works may be observed.

Below: On the same day standing on Lynmouth sea front at the foot of the cliff lift from Lynton is Western National No. **641** (**355 EDV**), a bus version of the Bristol SUL4A. It was about to set off for the climb up Countisbury Hill and over Porlock to Minehead.

Above: Across Exmoor and into Someset lies Porlock, two miles from which is Porlock Weir with its neat little harbour, by the side of which stood Western National No. **1619** (**LTA 778**), a Bristol LWL6B, in May 1958. It is about to return to Minehead via Porlock.

Below: Minehead was the location at one time of one of Butlin's giant holiday camps. The Western National garage is the location for a number of views depicting buses allocated by the company to the town. Not all the photographs taken on this visit were on dry days; this rather wet May 1958 picture shows Western National No. **218** (**ADV 124**), a 1936 Bristol J with postwar Beadle body.

Above: Evidence that not all Southern/Western National coaches were in Royal Blue livery was instanced by Western National No. **1302** (**LTA 740**), a Bristol LL6B with attractive Duple 37-seat coachwork. It is also seen at the garage at Minehead in May 1958, but in an altogether sunnier view.

Below: Brand new in the Royal Blue fleet at this time was No. **2228** (**XUO 711**), a Bristol MW6G with Eastern Coach Works body. The MW chassis had been introduced the previous year. The coach was parked outside Minehead garage.

Above: A bus of an altogether different generation pictured at Minehead Pier waiting to return to Exeter in June 1931 was Devon General **DV 9337**, an AEC Regal with Park Royal 32-seat body, new that year. The bus passed to Greenslades of Exeter in 1938.

Below: Found outside Minehead Station in 1958 was Western National No. **1743** (**RTT 953**) a 1955 Bristol LS5G, a model that was replaced by the MW. Today the station is the terminus of the West Somerset Railway, a heritage line which provides a steam-hauled service to Bishops Lydeard.

Back to the pier at Minehead and a look at Western National's double-deck operation in the area in the late 1950s. The upper picture shows No. **1824 (LTA 843)**, a Bristol KSW6B with lowbridge ECW 55-seat body new in 1951, while the lower view shows No. **1932 (UOD 486)**, a Bristol LD6B of 1957, the model which replaced the KSW. The advantage of the new model was, thanks to a dropped rear axle, its ability to combine a central gangway in the upper deck without increasing overall height when compared to the KSW, which required a sunken off-side gangway on the upper deck and consequent restricted headroom on the off-side of the lower deck. The buses are both waiting to set off on trunk services across Somerset, to Bridgewater and Taunton respectively.

Above: A final return to Minehead garage in May 1958. In the background may be seen former Leyland Titan No. **2848** converted for use as a tree-lopper. Number **1626** (**LTA 785**), a Bristol LWL6B shows Dunster on its service 296 destination display, which is as good a reason as any to visit this village in our next picture.

Below: Dunster, which also has a station on the West Somerset Railway, is a medieval Somerset town on the edge of Exmoor whose fame and wealth was built on cloth-making. The octagonal wooden Yarn Market in the High Street, seen in the background, was built in 1609. The coach was built 340 years later; **KLA 90** was an AEC Regal with Strachan body. It belonged to Thomas Tilling (BTC) of London, the parent company of which had been the owners of Western and Southern National until 1948. On the front it proclaims that it was operating a tour of Devon and Cornwall; while not yet there, Dunster undoubtedly had its attractions.

Above: Saving the best for last? It was impossible not to use this 1928 picture of Weston-super-Mare with the Bristol Tramways & Carriage Company's 1923 Bristol 3-ton registered **HT 8171** parked across the road from the then new bus station.

Below: All of the Royal Blue coaches seen so far in this book post date the sale of the company by Elliott Bros of Bournemouth. **RU 6728** was an ADC 424, new to Royal Blue in 1928, which on the purchase of the company by Southern/Western National in 1935 actually passed to Hants & Dorset. It is seen here at Wells prior to the sale.